THE THREE UNCLES
THE COLE BROTHERS IN THE GREAT WAR

T.L. Blackman

THE CHOIR PRESS

3302780048

First published in the United Kingdom in 2014 by
The Choir Press

ISBN 978-1-909300-23-1

For the great grandchildren of Michael William Cole:
Sheldon, Sarah, Thomas, Kaito and Shima,
and to the memory of Michael William Cole,
1917 – 2009.

CONTENTS

LIST OF PLATES

(*Copyright remains with the individual/organisation in italics*)

1. Mr Fritz and Mrs Rosamund Cole (nee Davies) on their wedding day (*Private Collection*)
2. The Cole Family, c. 1875 (*Private Collection*)
3. Cole and Lewis blotter (*Private Collection*)
4. Mrs Kitty Cole, wife of William Cole, with one of her children (*Private Collection*)
5. William Cole with daughter Irene (*Private Collection*)
6. Fritz William (F.W.) Cole (*Private Collection*)
7. 5th Battalion Gloucestershire Regiment, 1915 (*Soldiers of Gloucestershire Museum*)
8. Cyril Lawson Cole (*Marlborough College*)
9. Clifford Spearing Cole (*Marlborough College*)
10. Commissioning Scroll for Clifford Spearing Cole, 29 October 1914 (*Private Collection*)
11. Letters from the Western Front (*Private Collection*)
12. The gravestone of Clifford Cole, Royal Irish Rifles Graveyard, Laventie (*Private Collection*)
13. Telegram home regarding F.W. Cole (*Private Collection*)
14. The wedding of Mr and Mrs F.W. Cole, 13 September 1916 (*Private Collection*)
15. Maxwell Gerard Cole (*Marlborough College*)
16. Postcard from 2Lt M.G. Cole (*Private Collection*)
17. 1 Squadron, Ballieul, March 1917 (*Cross and Cockade International*)
18. 2Lt Lindsay Drummond (*Royal Military College of Canada*)
19. Memorial Plaque to Maxwell Gerard Cole (*Private Collection*)
20. Rosemund Cole and baby Michael (*Private Collection*)
21. 2/5th Gloucestershire Transport Section (*Soldiers of Gloucestershire Museum*)
22. The wedding of Mr and Mrs C.L. Cole, 23 November 1918 (*Private Collection*)
23. Medals of Major F.W. Cole (*Private Collection*)
24. Major F.W. Cole, c. 1950 (*Private Collection*)
25. Plan of Etaples Military Cemetery (*Commonwealth War Graves Commission*)
26. Plan of Oosttaverne Military Cemetery (*Commonwealth War Graves Commission*)
27. Plan of Royal Irish Rifles Military Cemetery, Laventie (*Commonwealth War Graves Commission*)

Mr Fritz and Mrs Rosamund Cole (nee Davies) on their wedding day

ACKNOWLEDGEMENTS

I am extremely grateful to the following individuals and organisations who helped with advice and information during the process of researching this book. I have received enormous support from my extended family (they know who they are) and special mention must go to Mrs Kay Cole and Mrs Jacky Middleton. Mrs Annie Blackman completed the first reading and also encouraged me.

The research was helped a great deal by Mr David Read from the Soldiers of Gloucestershire Museum, Dr T. Rogers from Marlborough College, Mr Andy Kemp from Cross and Cockade International and the hard-working staff at the National Archives (UK), the RAF Museum London, the Commonwealth War Graves Commission and Auckland Libraries. Also helpful with research were the many contributors to discussion boards on the internet, particularly those on ancestry.com and theaerodrome.com. Thank you also to Mrs Shelley Grey who helped me with British history and Kyle and Paula Williams who travelled with us to visit the graves in France. I am especially grateful to Paul and Paola Dashwood for the layout and cover design. My eternal gratitude goes to Iain, Sarah and Thomas who always support my projects. Any factual errors within this text are mine. Should any person discover a possible inaccuracy, I would be most appreciative if they could get in touch.

I will now borrow some words from another ancestor, Stamford Raffles Flint, author and editor of *The Mudge Memoirs* (1883). I have approached this research 'respectfully, ever mindful to the memory of those whom they record. It is with deference I put forward this book, so unskilfully handled, and intended originally for those to whom it would be of family or personal interest, trusting that whoever takes it up will treat it with lenience and consideration.'

And lastly, to my great-great grandparents, William and Kitty. Your boys have not been forgotten.

The Cole Family, c. 1875. Standing left to right: Alice Mary (born 1860), William Cole, Sarah Selina Cole (née Spearing),
William Henry Cole (1852), Sarah Ann (1849), Emma (1856), Arthur Abel (1854). Seated left to right: Margaret Mabel (1865), Harriet Augusta (1859),
Horace Ward (1870), Caleb Bruce (1862), Lillian Kathleen (1867), George Spearing (1858) and Florence Edith (1863)

Cole and Lewis blotter

PREFACE

Some people asked if this book was researched because of the First World War centenary. The truth is this journey began in July 2009 during Michael Cole's funeral. He was a popular man and St Dominic's, the large church at Camberwell in Melbourne, was full for his requiem mass. During the eulogy his wife of forty years, Mrs Kay Cole, referred to his father, Fritz Cole, as being 'lucky enough to be sent home after being injured on the Somme' and his three brothers not being so lucky as they were killed in France. Although we have always known that three of my grandfather's uncles died in the First World War, we knew very little of what actually happened to them. If someone did not research and write down the Cole's experiences then another generation would go by and the opportunity might be lost.

The research uncovered a family saga detailing the lives, adventures and tragic deaths of three of the four brave young Cole brothers. The story travels from the Somme, to the skies above the Western Front; from the Battle of Passchendaele, to the town of Brimscombe, Gloucestershire where dreaded telegrams would arrive. It includes, miraculously, survivable plane crashes in flimsy aircraft and lots of mud and vermin in the trenches. It is also a story of love, engagement, marriage and a baby, all set amid the backdrop of a war that seemed to have no end. The Coles were an ordinary family yet the research uncovered is an extraordinary story.

Kitty Cole, wife of William Cole, with one of her children

William Cole with daughter Irene

Chapter 1

MOBILISATION

Cole and Lewis (Bacon Curers) had been founded by William Cole and business partner Thomas Lewis in 1866. In 1883 their respective sons, William Henry Cole and Henry Thomas Lewis, were formally introduced into the partnership. William Henry married Catherine Martha White, known as Kitty, in 1888 and they initially lived at 22 Watermoor Road, Cirencester, Gloucestershire. By 1901 they had moved to Quern's Lane House, Cirencester. During these years they had seven children: four boys and three girls. The family had live-in servants including a governess, cook and several maids.

By 1911 William Henry Cole's oldest son, Fritz, had started working as a clerk in his father's office, and in about 1914 the family moved to Bourne House, Brimscombe. Fritz (23) still worked in the family business and was also a Territorial, being a 2nd Lieutenant in the 5th Gloucestershire Regiment. Cyril (21) was very academically inclined and as a graduate from the Engineering Faculty of Glasgow University with a Bachelor of Science degree had started an apprenticeship at the Fairfield Shipbuilding Yards in Glasgow. Clifford (18) had recently graduated from Marlborough College, Wiltshire, and Maxwell (16) was still boarding at Marlborough College as his three older brothers had before him. The three girls were Irene, known as Rene (25), Gwen (20) and Phyllis (13).

On 4 August 1914 thousands of telegrams were delivered throughout England including one to Fritz William Cole. The telegram contained one word, 'Mobilise'.

Germany had invaded Belgium. As an ally of Belgium, this meant that Britain was now at war with Germany. Fritz, as an existing member of the 5th Territorial Battalion, was immediately sent to Chelmsford, in Essex, for training. There was a huge influx of volunteers wanting to join the 5th Gloucestershire Regiment and it had to be divided into two groups, known as the 1/5th and 2/5th. Fritz was part of the 1/5th (pronounced "first fifth") Gloucestershire Regiment, and according to the Soldiers of Gloucestershire Museum (SOGM), these soldiers were the 'cream of the crop'. On 2 September 1914 Fritz was promoted to Captain. The 1/5th Battalion, Gloucestershire Regiment, was part of the 145th Brigade, 48th (South Midland) Division. Their final training was undertaken far from home in Danbury, near Chelmsford.

During this time Fritz began corresponding with Margaret Rosamund Davies, known as Rosamund or Wommie. She was the daughter of the Rev Charles Douglas Percy Davies.[1] Her mother was Jessie Mudge, the great-great granddaughter of Thomas Mudge, a famous clockmaker.[2] Rosamund had a sister, Dorothie and two brothers Home (pronounced Hume)

Fritz William Cole

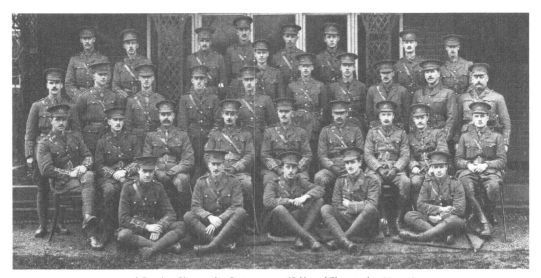

5th Battalion Gloucestershire Regiment, 1915 (Soldiers of Gloucestershire Museum)
1st Row:- Lt. R.M.F. Cooke, Capt. R.S.D. Stuart, 2nd Lt. W. Vaughan, Lt. F.E. Francillon, Lt. L.R.C. Sumner, 2nd Lt. H.S. King,
Capt. H.C.B. Sessions, Lt. H.P. Snowden
2nd Row:- Capt. A.T. Mitcheson, 2nd Lt. C.F.R. Barnett, 2nd Lt. H.G.C. Guise, Lt. G.A. Lister, Lt. W. Frean, Lt. F. Balfour, 2nd Lt. E. Conder,
2nd Lt. E.F.G. Brenan, 2nd Lt. T.H. Moore, Lt. F.H. Sprague, R.A.M.C., Lt. & Q.M.C.F. Foote.
3rd Row:- Capt. G.F. Collett, Capt. R.J. Caruthers Little, Capt. H. Hague, Major J.F. Tarrant, Lt-Col. J.H. Collett, Capt. & Adj. V.N. Johnson,
Major N.H. Waller, Capt. Visct. Campden, Capt. F.W. Cole.
4th Row:- 2nd Lt. A.J. Dodgson, 2nd Lt. C.W. Winterbotham, 2nd Lt. J.A. Case, 2nd Lt. L.W. Moore, 2nd Lt. C.S. Nason.

and John who was known to the family as Jack. Fritz wrote to Rosamund on 11 November,

> *'It was horribly hard sleeping on the ground and worse still when I had to go on*
> *to a hard floor and no mattress.'*

Records supplied by the SOGM, including private diaries, tell that the men practised their foot and rifle drill, were fitted with uniforms and speculated where they would be sent. The uniforms were most unpopular as the belt and leather straps were very difficult to get on and off owing to an awkward design feature and were very heavy even without the rounds of ammunition that would eventually have to be carried. After rumours of India, Egypt and Italy, a particular immunisation near Christmas led the soldiers to suspect France was their destination.

About this time the 2/5th Gloucestershire Regiment was also formed and both Cyril and Clifford signed up immediately. Establishing a new regiment from scratch was a monumental task and several officers were transferred from the 1/5th Battalion to facilitate this. There were no uniforms. As men from all walks of life were recruited they would turn up to their training dressed in civilian clothes and were identified as a member of the 2/5th Gloucesters by a white silk ribbon pinned to their coat. The Cole brothers were all confident horse riders. Like the men, the horses had been recruited from civilian life and included ex-racehorses and mules. Some of the men had little experience with horses and lacked confidence as riders. Particularly nervous individuals were given to 'Old Tom', an ex-milk delivery mount, who refused to hurry in any situation and through force of habit stopped at every single gate causing chaos when the men were marching in columns. By the end of the year the men had their uniforms and were ready for the next stage of their military training. In February 1915 the 2/5th Battalion left for Northampton, as there were other regiments there and it gave them a chance to train as part of a larger group. In April they returned to Chelmsford. During the summer of 1915 Zeppelins raided England often and twice dropped bombs on Chelmsford. Owing to their education, both Cyril and Clifford were promoted to Officers.

Clifford Spearing Cole (Marlborough College)

Cyril Lawson Cole (Marlborough College)

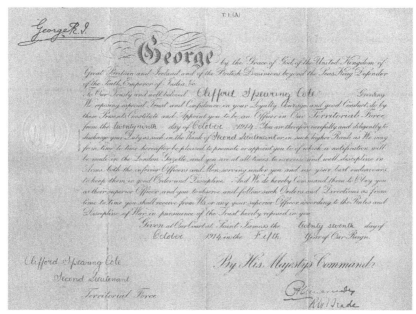

Commissioning Scroll for Clifford Spearing Cole

Chapter 2

FRITZ COLE IN THE TRENCHES

Early in 1915 His Majesty King George V visited the 1/5th Gloucestershire training camp. In March the soldiers were instructed to pack up all their private possessions to be transported back to their homes so that all they were left with was their official kit. Thankfully, the bulky leather straps and belts were replaced with much more comfortable ones made of khaki webbing.

The 1/5th Battalion Gloucestershire Regiment left England at 9pm on 29th March 1915, crossing the channel under bright moonlight on RMS Invicta and landing at Boulogne, France at 11pm. They marched some way to a French camp where they were allocated tents but got little sleep owing to a bitterly cold northerly wind. The next day, after travelling by cattle truck (30 soldiers to a truck) and another long march, the Battalion arrived at Steenvorde, Belgium on 30th March. They were assigned to the Ploegsteert Wood sector and billeted out in barns and lofts.

As an officer, Fritz was responsible for receiving orders from above and then coordinating his men to carry out those orders. British soldiers on the front line worked to a timetable of sixteen days. Eight days in front-line trenches, four days in reserve trenches then four days resting in a temporary camp a few miles back. The term 'resting' is perhaps a misnomer, as the days were spent with early starts and hard work – quite different from being on leave, which only occurred on rare occasions. The sixteen-day timetable was often lengthened, especially during times when extended manpower was needed. Rations were carried long distances, often in hessian bags and the condition of the food would sometimes deteriorate before arrival, particularly if it has been raining. Army biscuits, jam and bully beef were prepared by men in various imaginative ways to try and give some semblance of variety.

The horror of the trenches is best described by those that were there. Some soldiers kept diaries, including Henry Buckle. He was also a talented artist and his account, 'A Tommy's Sketchbook', is very revealing about the daily life in France of those in the 1/5th Gloucestershire Regiment. He writes:

> *3 sentries continually ears and eyes alert over that vacant 80 yards. 3 of us*
> *share a dug-out which is about 3 feet high, 5 feet long and about 5 wide.*
> *A bag over the 'front door', which is a yard square, enables a candle to be lit*
> *inside to see to write (as now) or to get a meal. Shall have to be about all night,*
> *for have charge of this particular bit of trench.*

Letters from the Western Front

The trenches had sandbags on the walls and boards on the floor. In between the German trenches and the Allied trenches was an area known as No Man's Land. There was a constant battle with mud, sickness, vermin, lice and rats. To deter illness, drinking water was heavily treated with chloride. Fritz's role as an officer included endless paperwork, organising rations, ammunition and physically leading his men over the top.

The highlight of Fritz's day was reading letters from home and writing to his sweetheart Rosamund. He kept her letters in his suitcase. They were tied with one of her cherry-coloured hair ribbons along with her photograph in a small frame that he would look at while writing to her. He wrote to other family members too but often felt guilty that he didn't write to them more frequently due to writing to his dearest 'Wommie' every single day. There was no privacy. All letters were censored by the Army before being mailed back to England. Here is an excerpt from a letter he wrote to Rosamund's mother, Mrs Jessie Davies.

> *1/5th Glos Regt.*
> *1st S.M. Div*
> *B.E.F.*
> *Tuesday 20/4/1915*
>
> *We came out of the trenches last night after 4 days and nights and are about 2 miles from the front line, resting.*
>
> *It is an awful strain, as naturally one doesn't get much sleep, and what one does get is not very restful, with all the bustle and noise all the time. The first night was rather an ordeal and I didn't sleep a wink until after dawn, as I felt the responsibility too great. Nevertheless by the 4th day I seemed quite used to it, but was very thankful to get away for a rest ...*
> *... All I want now is for the war to finish so that I can come back to Wommie again ...*
> *... We had a sad thing happen yesterday afternoon. One of our subalterns was shot through the head and killed instantly. He was such a cheerful fellow and a perfect dear and absolutely without fear. However we shall have to get used to all this, but it is very sad.*

At this time, Fritz was second in command of C Company. After a quiet day in the trenches on 4th May there was much activity during the night from the enemy snipers and machine guns. According to the SOGM this was interspersed with the enemy shouting from their trenches 'Shut Up Gloucesters' and 'England kaput!'.

In July 1915, Fritz was transferred to Le Havre to coordinate reinforcements to the Brigade that were arriving from England. He rejoined the 1/5th Gloucesters in September as acting commanding officer of D Company, where he and his men alternated time in the trenches at Hébuterne with billets in the nearby villages of Bus and Sailly.

In December 1915, while on leave, Fritz wrote another letter to Mrs Davies:

> *Tues Dec. 21st*
>
> *... I am heaps and heaps better and have been out for a walk this morning, only it was so horribly wet that I didn't stay out very long.*
> *I rejoin the Regt. tomorrow morning, and I shall be glad to see them again. All the same I have had a lovely rest here and I am sure it has done me lots of good. I have had two letters from them since I have been in here, which was ripping, as naturally I am continually wondering how they are getting on up in the trenches when I am not there.*
> *My leave has been ages coming around again, hasn't it? but it is so lovely to have it to look forward to always.*

To view a map of the Western Front in 1915 visit http://www.thethreeuncles.com

Chapter 3

LIFE IN FRANCE

The Royal Flying Corps had been formed on 13 April 1912 as a division of the British Army. The primary role of aircraft at this time was to support the PBI (Poor Bloody Infantry) in the trenches below them. Besides the traditional air balloons there was a new invention – airplanes. The Wright Brothers had flown at Kitty Hawk in the world's first documented controlled flight in 1903 followed by the first crossing of the English Channel from Calais to Dover by Louis Blériot in 1909, merely five years before the outbreak of war. Aircraft were mass produced for the war effort and the technological advances were rapid at that time. Two seater planes carried a pilot and an observer whose prime responsibility was to gain intelligence on what was happening over enemy lines. This included the taking of photographs. Sometimes scout planes carrying a single pilot defended the area so the pilot and observer could carry out their tasks.

On Wednesday 9th February 1916 Fritz wrote,

> *We have been out since 11 o'clock this morning, on a visit to a neighbouring squadron of the Flying Corps, & we had a very interesting day. We all hoped to get a joyride, but when we got there, we were told that there was only one ride for every 12 of us, so we had to toss for it. Kerwood won it, & he was up for about 15 minutes. It must have been just lovely, as it was a clear afternoon, tho' terribly cold. He enjoyed it very much, and of course the rest of us were rather sick, because we couldn't go as well. We saw some very interesting things and arrived back here at 5 o'clock, very hungry and awfully cold because of the snow on the ground.*

On 23rd February 1916 the Battalion arrived at Hébuterne. D Company, still led by Acting Commander, Captain Fritz Cole, were in Trenches XVII to XXI inclusive. During this period on the front line, D Company also spent a lot of time in an area of trenches known as The Keep.

On 3 April 1916 Fritz wrote to Rosamund,

> *Last night I slept in a pig sty, and very comfy it was too. I had a box mattress fixed up there and it has all been cleaned out and disinfected; it has been used by officials before for some time, only the bed wasn't there. F'allon slept in the pig sty next to mine.*

On 9th April, Fritz returned to England on leave and spent valuable time with his family. Fritz and Rosamund became engaged to be married. He almost certainly would have asked her father, the Rev Charles P. Davies, for permission. Due to the nature of the times and their Christian faith, Fritz and Rosamund weren't able to spend as much time alone as they would have wished. To have any kind of privacy, they would need to be married, but they didn't want a 'war wedding' and many people still thought the war wasn't going to last much longer.

Fritz was disappointed to be called back to the front on 19th April as it was two days earlier than expected. On the same day that he returned to the Battalion, Fritz was given the news that after having been Acting Commander of "D" Company for some time he was now permanently in the role. There was also a revealing entry in the Battalion War Diary that day regarding the constant danger the men were in.

19th April: 'Situation quiet. Casualties: 2 Other Ranks wounded.'

On Sunday 7th May 1916 Fritz wrote to Rosamund,

> *Thank you so much for your dear letter yesterday. I got it as I was walking down the village, on my way to my bath. I sat and read it as the orderly was getting the bath ready for me. Of course one can never tell, but by my next leave, the war may seem to be much nearer the end, than it does at present and for your sake I don't want a war wedding. All the same if it goes on at the present rate, and seems like going on for another year I don't think I could wait an indefinite time like that ...*

In another letter on 10th May he seems frustrated.

> *I expected to be gone from here by now, but late last night orders were suddenly altered and we aren't going till this evening. In consequence, the post cart will not come up, but our letters will be waiting for us, when we get back, but I don't suppose we shall be in time to catch the post out. It is so rotten when orders are suddenly altered like that, as it means a double dose of work, and all your arrangements have to be made all over again. It does mean such a lot to do.*

On 11 May 1916, Rosamund's younger brother Home wrote from boarding school at Haileybury College in Hertford. Like the rest of the family he called her by her nickname, Wommie.

> *You can't think how pleased I am to hear you are engaged. I simply leapt for joy when I opened your letter, It's the very best piece of news I have ever had ever since I have been alive and I can't say more than that ... Always your very loving brother, Home.*

Fritz's letters home weren't particularly newsy owing to the constant overseeing eye of the censor. His routine in late May was described in a letter home to Rosamund. Breakfast was at 5.45am followed by a route march at 6.30am. The route march was done early to get it over with in the cool of the morning and the men were back by 11am. Lunch followed, then at 2pm Fritz had to supervise the mess (kitchen/dining area) being packed up in practice for when the Battalion next moved. He knew Rosamund would be pleased to get this letter because they were back from the front line for a short rest. Although the men had long busy days, their lives were not so directly at risk.

June was relatively quiet as 145th Brigade (including 1/5th Battalion) spent most of their time in the town of Sailly au Bois and surrounding villages 'in reserve'. He wrote to Rosamund on the 10th June that the men had been on a march to a new town in the pouring rain. Although he particularly despised getting soaked through, he did enjoy one aspect of a march. He added, 'It's a lovely time for thinking, as whether I am walking or riding, I am alone at the head of my company.'

10th June 1916 is the same day that 2/5th Gloucestershire Regiment, including Cyril and Clifford Cole, arrived at Laventie. Clifford had arrived on the ship HMT 861 in Le Havre on 25th May 1916. The ship contained 30 Officers and 786 Other Ranks. Cyril was in the transport division which travelled on the SS Inventor with the Brigade Headquarters. The Battalion had camped and been billeted in towns including Le Sart and Reiz Bailleul on the way to Laventie where the men prepared to enter the trenches for the first time.

Three of the four Cole brothers were now in France.

The gravestone of Clifford Cole, Royal Irish Rifles Graveyard, Laventie

Chapter 4

2/5TH GLOUCESTERSHIRE REGIMENT

On 15 June 1916 the 2/5th Gloucestershire Battalion had their first experience of trench duty in the Fauquissart-Laventie Sector. It was an eventful first week. On 18th June, Lt. Clifford Cole was promoted to Captain. The very next day, he was the first officer from the Battalion to lose his life when he was killed by an aerial torpedo.

In his book 2/5th Battalion Gloucestershire Regiment 1914 – 1918, A.F. Barnes (MC) relates,

> *He had been with [the Battalion] since its early days and by his efficiency and good nature he had won the esteem of both officers and men. His death, taking place so soon after the Battalion had gone to France, came as a blow.*

Later that week there was a raid on the Germans by A Company of 2nd/5th Gloucesters led by Captain Wales. Once the men had gone over the top, it became apparent that the wire in No Man's Land had not been cut through properly, holding the men up. The Germans took advantage of the situation by subjecting them to merciless machine-gun fire. The British retreated back to their own trench after suffering serious casualties. There were many acts of bravery during the raid and several awards were granted including a Military Cross to Captain Wales.

Four hundred and sixty-three soldiers lie today at Royal Irish Rifles Graveyard in Laventie. Six 2nd/5th Gloucestershire graves lie side by side in row II.J.

> *Pte. J. Hall, II.J.1, 21June16, Age 22*
> *Pte. CW. Jackson, II.J.2, 21 June 16, Age 19*
> *Pte. F. Yeldham, II.J.3, 21 June 16, Age 39*
> *Pte. E. Skellern, II.J.4, 20 June 16, Age 20*
> *Lt. C. Cole, II.J.5, 19 June 16, Age 20*
> *Pte. W. Phipps, II.J.6, 20 June 16, Age unknown*

Families of soldiers of other ranks were informed by post that their loved one had been killed. This consisted of a standard army form with details handwritten in blank spaces. Because Clifford was an Officer, the Cole family back home in Brimscombe would have been informed of his death by telegram as soon as possible.

The Cole family composed an obituary for an unknown publication. A draft hand-written copy is in the family papers:

> *Clifford Spearing Cole joined up on the outbreak of War and obtained his commission in the Gloucestershire Regt in Sept 1914, being posted to the 2nd 5th Batt. with his brother. He proceeded to France in April 1916 soon transferring to the Trench Mortars. He was killed by an aerial Torpedo on June 19th 1916 whilst in command of his battery, having been granted his Captaincy on the day previous to his death.*

Chapter 5

BATTLE OF THE SOMME

Fritz remained in the trenches in Hébuterne until July and the Battle of the Somme. The 1/5th Gloucestors were transferred to Sailly au Bois and from 14 July they were heavily involved in the attack on Ovillers.

On 23rd July 1916, at 12.35am the 145b Infantry Brigade (including 1/5 Glocesters) and 144 Infantry Brigade was ordered to attack. The Battalion War Diary (SOGM) reads in part:

> *"A" Company on Right – "C" on left – "B" in support – "D" in reserve. The attack was quickly discovered by enemy who were holding all trenches strongly. Heavy barrage of artillery and machine gun fire were opened and in spite of being reinforced by "B" Company the objectives were not reached. A fresh attack after new bombardment of 10 minutes by our guns opposite "A" Company's objective also failed. Stokes guns and oil bombs from mortars were used during preliminary bombardment.*

One Officer died and seven others, including Fritz and Lt H.S. King (known to the Cole family as Harry), were wounded. Casualties in other ranks included 12 killed, 23 missing and 113 wounded. After three hours of fighting, the 145 Brigade was relieved by the 1/1st Buckingham Battalion from Oxford and the Bucks Light Infantry who went on to capture the trenches, two machine guns and 120 enemy who surrendered.

On 26th July, a telegram was delivered to the Cole family home in Brimscombe which read:

> *T/4551 regret to inform you Capt. FW Cole 5th Glosters Regt admitted one Red Cross Hospital. Le Touquet 24th July gunshot wound elbow.*

Fritz was immediately sent back to England to recover. On 13 September 1916, Fritz and Rosamund were married at Fretherne, Gloucestershire where the Davies family lived.

Once married, Fritz and Rosamund moved to a small flat in the city of Bath near where Fritz had been sent to train officers at Prior Park. Although he was considered medically unfit to return to the front, family history relates that this may have been due to being badly gassed in the trenches rather than the wound on his elbow referred to in the telegram.

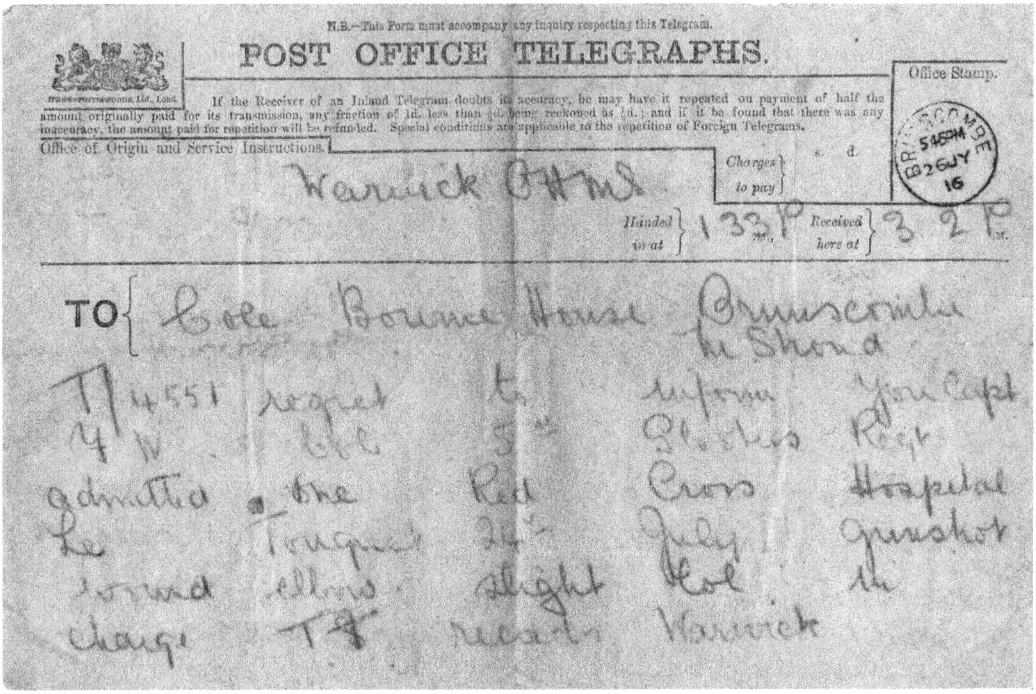
N.B.—This Form must accompany any inquiry respecting this Telegram.

POST OFFICE TELEGRAPHS.

Office Stamp.

If the Receiver of an Inland Telegram doubts its accuracy, he may have it repeated on payment of half the amount originally paid for its transmission, any fraction of 1d. less than ½d. being reckoned as ½d.; and if it be found that there was any inaccuracy, the amount paid for repetition will be refunded. Special conditions are applicable to the repetition of Foreign Telegrams.

Office of Origin and Service Instructions. Warwick OHMS

Charges to pay s. d.

BRIMSCOMBE 5 45PM 26 JY 16

Handed in at 133P Received here at 3 2 P M.

TO Cole Bourne House Brimscombe Nr Stroud

T/4551 regret to inform you Capt F W Cole 5th Glosters Regt admitted the Red Cross Hospital Le Touquet 24th July Gunshot wound elbow slight Col in charge T F records Warwick

Telegram home regarding F.W. Cole

On 1 July 1916, the first day of the Battle of the Somme, there were 57,000 British casualties including 19,000 killed. The battle finally ended on 18th November due to overnight snow. Over the previous five months the Allies had advanced 8 miles over a 20-mile front line at a cost of 420,000 British and 200,000 French lives. Half a million Germans lives were also lost. To see a copy of a map of the Somme in 1916 visit www.thethreeuncles.com

'The Cross of Wood' was composed by Lt Cyril William Winterbotham, C Company 1st/5th Battalion, Gloucestershire Regiment. Lt Winterbotham composed this poem in early July 1916 while in the trenches at Hébuterne (Powell, 2006). It was first published in London in November 1917 and reprinted in February 1918 in *The Muse in Arms, a Collection of War Poems*, edited by E.B. Osborn. Lt Winterbotham was killed on 27 August 1916 at Ovillers during an attack on a German trench while in command of C Company. He is one of the officers in the group photograph of 1/5th Gloucestershire Officers.

'The Cross of Wood'
God be with you and us who go our way
And leave you dead upon the ground you won;
For you at last the long fatigue is done,
The hard march ended, you have rest to-day.

You were our friends with you we watched the dawn
Gleam through the rain of the long winter night,
With you we laboured till the morning light
Broke on the village, shell-destroyed and torn.

Not now for you the glorious return
To steep Stroud valleys, to the Severn leas
By Tewkesbury and Gloucester, or the trees
Of Cheltenham under high Coltswold stern.

For you no medals such as others wear –
A cross of bronze for those approved brave –
To you is given, above a shallow grave,
The Wooden Cross that marks you resting there.

Rest you content, more honourable far
Than all the Orders is the Cross of Wood,
The symbol of self-sacrifice that stood
Bearing the God whose brethren you are.

Mr and Mrs F.W. Cole's wedding day 13 September 1916, Standing: Brian S. Cole, Captain ?, Rev Charles Davies, Jack Davies, Maxwell Cole, Fritz Cole, Harry King, Home Davies, Mr W.H. Cole, Captain B. Little, Phyllis Cole. Seated: Freda Cockey, Mrs Jessie Davies, Rosamund, Mrs C. Cole, Rene Cole. On Ground: Dorothie Davies, Gwen Cole, Marjorie Grayling (née Wheatley)

Chapter 6

THE ROYAL FLYING CORPS

While Fritz was on the Somme, and Cyril was further north, their youngest brother, Maxwell Gerard Cole, was about to graduate from school. Born at Quern's Lane House in Cirencester on 28th May 1898 and educated initially at Glengarth, Cheltenham, in September 1912 he enrolled at Marlborough College where he, like his three elder brothers before him, joined Junior House A2. During his time at school Maxwell was a member of Marlborough College's Officers Training Corps. The college records show that in February 1916 he was promoted to 'Corporal', and further promoted in May 1916 to 'Sergeant'.

In July of 1916 Maxwell left Marlborough College and applied to the army for an Appointment to the Special Reserve of Officers. He was granted Second Lieutenant Land Forces in August 1916 and accepted to the General List and Christ Church College for instruction in aviation. Maxwell spent time in Croydon, Surrey during his training with No. 17 Reserve Squadron and graduated with his Pilot's Certificate in December 1916.

His cousin, Brian Spearing Cole, who initially trained with 12th Gloucestershire Regiment in 1914, had later joined the Royal Flying Corps and trained as a pilot in Filton, near Bristol. Brian's training was with 66 Squadron from 8 September until 6 November 1916. Late in 1916 Brian transferred to No. 1 Squadron which was stationed in a building previously used as a lunatic asylum in Bailleul, a town in northern France close to Belgium.

Max sent a postcard to Fritz on 19 October 1916 from Croydon.

> *My Dear Fritz*
> *How are you old man, I am glad to hear you are better, I think married life must be a great tonic. Wendy, Harry & Kath came over to the aerodrome this morning. I saw three little flies crawling along the road and guessed it was them. Wendy is looking awfully well so is Harry.*
> *Best love to all. Max*

The Wendy referred to in the postcard is Gwen Cole (sister to Max and Fritz) and Harry is Harry King who was wounded with Fritz during the attack on Ovillers.

In January 1917 Maxwell was attached to No. 1 AD (Aircraft Depot) in St-Omer, France, about 25 miles from No. 1 Squadron at Bailleul. However, on 28 January Brian Cole was seriously injured in a plane crash and so, by the time Maxwell was posted to No. 1 Squadron

Maxwell Gerard Cole

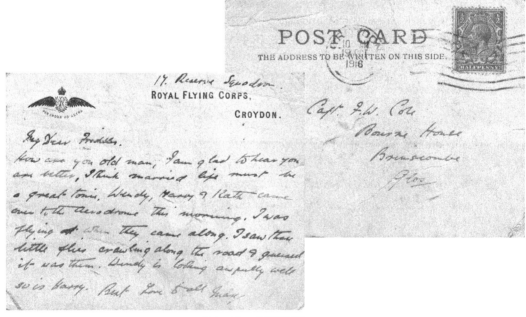

Postcard from 2Lt M.W. Cole

on 3 February 1917, Brian was no longer there. According to Fritz in a letter to Rosamund a couple of months later, it was a wonder that Brian hadn't died, as he was executing a forced landing and couldn't find anywhere to land. He remembered very little of the incident except he saw a small field and tried to cover his face as the plane crashed. He regained consciousness to find himself under the plane covered in blood and in the longer term was left with a serious facial scar and very rattled nerves. However, he did recover and returned to the Royal Flying Corps as a fighter pilot at a later date.[3]

As explained earlier, two-seater planes carried a pilot and observer whose prime responsibility was to gain intelligence on what was happening over enemy lines including the taking of photographs. Scout planes carrying a single pilot defended the skies so the pilot and observer could carry out their tasks. At this time Germany held air superiority. Germany had taken the initiative to fund research and development into modern aircraft suitable for war while the British government had chosen to use funds elsewhere. This meant that by early 1917 British pilots were flying outdated planes and the average life expectancy for a new fighter pilot was less than two weeks. Shortly before Maxwell proceeded to France, No. 1 Squadron became a fighter squadron flying single-seater planes.

Lt Stewart Keith-Jopp, author of the highly informative chapter 'Twenty-Eight Days in France' in the Ninth Series of the 1930s periodical *Great War Adventures*, was a pilot in No. 1 Squadron at the same time as Maxwell and he describes the situation at Bailleul very well. Pilots who were transferred to No. 1 Squadron during this time had never flown single seater Nieuport planes before and accidents were commonplace. On 5 February, two days after arrival, Maxwell crashed his first plane, a Nieuport 17 with serial number A6618. It was wrecked during landing and initially written off. However, after being returned to the depot it was decided to reconstruct it.

From 17 to 24 February 1917 Max spent time at the School of Aerial Gunnery before returning to No. 1 Squadron. Then from 18 to 25 March he was on temporary duty to the 1. AD.

The Battle of Arras raged throughout April 1917. The death toll for pilots was terrible and the month has become known as Bloody April. No. 1 Squadron was not hit as badly as some other squadrons. Although parachutes were used by observers in kite balloons, they were not issued to pilots. It has been estimated that one third of lives lost at the front in planes could have been saved by the use of parachutes. Richard Townshend Bickers explains the Air Board's official stance in *The First Great Air War* (p. 175):

> *the presence of such an apparatus might impair the fighting spirit of pilots and cause them to abandon machines which might otherwise be capable of returning to base for repair.*

No. 1 Squadron, Bailleul, March 1917 (Photograph courtesy of Cross and Cockade International).
Back Row: Lt L.J. Mars, Lt J.A. Slater, Lt P.M. Le Gallais, Unknown, Third Row: Unknown, Unknown, Lt A.W. Wood, Unknown, Unknown, Lt R.J. Bevington. Second Row: 2Lt V.H. Collins, Capt R.H. Cronyn, Lt E.D. Atkinson, Major J.G. St P. De Dombasle, Lt C.J.Q. Brand, Unknown, Lt T.F. Hazell. Front Row: 2Lt E.M. Wright, 2Lt M.G. Cole, Lt S. McKercher, 2Lt E.S.T. Cole, Lt J.R. Anthony, 2Lt D. Macdonald, 2Lt L.M. Mansbridge

Michael Shaw included excepts of Lt Keith-Jopp's diary in *Twice Vertical* (1971, p.47). Keith-Jopp enjoyed dusk patrols and wrote the following in May 1917:

> *This evening we did a patrol beyond Menin. Suddenly our leader went into a spiral dive. We all followed. I was in the rear and it was beautiful watching the other five machines cascading down.*

He continues,

> *After going down about 6,000 ft, I saw several shadow machines against this blue and then suddenly a bright red machine dived through the shaft of light. For a second or two, it shone like a red flame and disappeared into the blue beyond. This was probably Richthofen and his circus, as they came up into our sector of the line that day. We followed them down some way, and then gave up."*

The Royal Flying Corps Communiqués were issued weekly by RFC headquarters (see Bowyer, 1998). They show that on 29 April 1917, hostile aircraft were driven down out of control by (among others) 2 Lt Cole, No. 1 Squadron. It is not known if this was Maxwell as there were two 2nd Lts Cole in the Squadron at that time. However, we do know that on the same day, according to Neiuports In RNAS, RFC and RAF Service, Maxwell crashed a second plane, Nieuport B1554, in a forced landing at Bray Dunes.

Further entries in the RFC Communiqués show 30 April 1917, '2nd Lt M G Cole, 1 Squadron, drove down a HA [hostile aircraft] out of control, then he and Capt E D Atkinson of the same squadron drove down two more out of control'; and on 1 May 1917, 'An Albatross scout which was engaged by 2nd Lt MG Cole, 1 Squadron was brought down in our lines near Elverdinghe.' On 2 May, Maxwell went on leave, returning on 16 May.

In early May 1917 there was a series of successful attacks on German observation balloons. The balloons were nicknamed German Sausages. The usual method was for fighter planes to fly in at great height then attack the balloons from the air by diving vertically and shooting the balloon from above. However, earlier in that month, 40 Squadron completed a successful surprise attack with a new technique of flying in very low then firing from below. This was much more dangerous as there was ground-based anti-aircraft artillery including machine guns protecting the balloons at all time.

On 9 May 1917, young pilot (eventually Major) 'Mick' Mannock from 40 Squadron wrote about this incident in his diary (F. Oughton (ed.),1966),

> *Went over the lines from north of Arras to five miles behind the German trenches at a height of less than fifteen feet, attacking Hun balloons. That was on the 7th – a Monday. Six of us – Captain Nixon (missing), Hall, Scudamore, Redler, Parry and myself. All except the Captain ... returned safely but with machines shot to pieces. Hall crashed on home aerodrome, as did Scudamore, Parry crashed just our side of the lines as the Canadian H.Q. Redler crashed at Savy, but returned here later and damaged his machine on landing. I was the only one to return properly to the aerodrome, and made a perfect landing. We all got our objectives. My fuselage had bullet holes in it, one very near my head, and the wings were more or less riddled. I don't want to go through such an experience again.*

Chapter 7

THE MUNITIONS MAN AND MEETING PERCY

After Fritz and Rosamund were married they lived together in Bath where Fritz was training officers at Prior Park. Rosamund very soon became pregnant. Fritz was working very long days and the pregnancy did not always go smoothly. After some months Rosamund moved back to her parents at Fretherne where, towards the end of her pregnancy, she was put on bed rest.

Of course, they wrote many letters. Fritz wrote from the Cole Family home, Bourne House, Brimscombe, on 12 March 1917 when Rosamund was about six months pregnant:

> *My own beloved Darling,*
> *I am starting my letter now, 9.45 before Franklin is ready to help me collect my things and pack, and as Mrs King and her eldest son Cyril are coming to lunch and tea, I don't suppose I shall have much chance later ...*

Mrs King was Harry King's mother and Cyril his elder brother. Harry had been wounded during the attack on Ovillers at the same time as Fritz. He goes on to relate news from his sister Wendy (Gwen) about their cousin Brian.

> *Wendy says that poor old Brian is quite disfigured on one side of his face, by a big scar which makes him have a dreadful sneer, isn't it sad? It is a wonder he wasn't killed, as he had a forced landing and nowhere to land. He came down in the corner of a little field and remembers nothing but trying to protect his face and then coming to, under the machine and covered with blood. His nerves are all over the place I believe poor fellow ...*

Fritz goes on to relate a tale which shows how life at home was the same yet different owing to the ongoing war.

> *It is about Ione. She has had a regular bust up with the Richards,⁴ Mother had a letter from Mrs Richards and she gave it to me to read, and I knew it would interest you. First of all, she decided to settle about 3 miles from the Richards in a huge house and garden called 'Something Hall' and was going to have a motor car to assist in her war work. Of course the Richards told her it was absolutely ridiculous but the more they tried to put her off doing it the*

keener she got. Then one day she went off to S'Hampton to do some shopping in the morning and by tea time had not returned. Of course the Richards were in an awful way and informed the police. She didn't return till 10pm when she walked in as large as life and quite calmly, having walked back from the town with a munitions man, a complete stranger. Then of course people began Talking, and her nurse has given notice. ... The upshot of the whole thing is that the Richards will have nothing more to do with her. ... They hint in the letter that they think she is an immoral woman. Isn't it awkward for Mother? She doesn't know what to do and doesn't like to believe it all and refuse to have her here.

The letter ends with travel arrangements which indicate that Fritz's work took him to other centres away from Prior Park.

Gardiner is coming here with Dad at 6 o'clock from Stonehouse at 7.56. Then I hope I shan't have to change again till York. Now I must go and do my affairs and then begin my packing. Love to your Pa and Ma and tell your Ma that I will write to her from Yorkshire (my bread and butter letter). With all my love and hugs and kisses for my very one and only little Girlie.
Ever your own loving hubby Fritz
N.B. What a lovely afternoon we had yesterday didn't we? You Darling!!!

With less than a month to go before her baby was due, Rosamund received a letter from her younger brother, Home (aged 20) who by this time had left college and was fighting in France.

128th Battery
R.F.A.
B.E.F. France
May 22, 1917

Dearest Wommie,

I reiterate the statement that you made at the beginning of your letter about not writing for a long time. Only in my case it's so long that I fear you will put my letter on one side as being some unpaid bill or other trivial matter owing to complete forgetfulness of my handwriting.

I'm sorry to hear that you're so ugly now. If I was you I would take to heart some of the advertisements in the cheaper magazines and invest in a maternity skirt or some other monstrosity.

But perhaps you're of the old fashioned school yet in your ideas, saying 'What matters to my face, form or figure, am I doing duty?' Alack! Your opinions on the subject are to me as a closed book and I am torn in the teeth of doubt as to what comments will be most to your liking.

What trees there are left out there to us by the wilful Hun are stretching out myriad hands of thankfulness to be allowed to see another Spring. In fact some that not so long ago were looking down in disgust and contempt upon trench raids and other atrocities are now so braced to be out of the danger zone that even they have perked up and protruded a snag of greenery from here and there. By this time I suppose Friddles will have gone again. He's almost like the other Fritz who we know but with whom we have no peaceful communication (for in the Army it corrupts good manners). Here today and gone tomorrow but he leaves his crumps behind him.

I met a most delightful Percy [5] tonight. He measured 25cms across his posterior portion. He possessed two (if you please) copper driving bands and had the most gigantically calibred head I have ever seen (about 20 calibres I should think). His snout was of the hardest steel imaginable and his posterior was ornamented by the fuse instead of carrying it on his snout as is usual. He was set to a delay of half a second and he had failed completely to disintegrate 'in other words' a dud. I did not meddle too much with him. Percy is apt to be fractious when he has failed his first time so I stopped and I looked and listened and I left. You spoke of leave I think in your epistle. Did you ever stand on Dartmoor – on one of its peaks – on a fine day in autumn with the air as clear as the water in mid-ocean? Did you look across to the peak the other side and think 'Ah that's not far. Perhaps I'll walk across and then find that it's three miles? Well the clear air is the seven months or so leaveless which leads you to think that the further valley – the haven where you would be – can not be far now.

And it's just as deceitful, all the more so as the white heather that you have sought for many months lies the other side and is as clear in your eyes as home is in mine.

What do you think of this as an effort? Another fellow and myself composed it tonight. We're rather proud of it

It approached me with velocity gigantic
It's speed was quite commensurate with sound
It's sibilations bordered on the frantic
Vibrations went pulsating through the ground
It landed with a brobdinagian wallop
My Cardiac organ quivered at the thud
But if failed completely in disintegration
In other words – a dud.

It is the beginning of a great Epic entitled 'Ode on the failure of Percy to do his duty'
I think that by now this letter has reached its terminus as far as you're concerned and you deserve one no longer. Be thankful for that you have.
Tons of love from Home.

Chapter 8

WHAT HAPPENED ON 18 MAY 1917?

"Onward Baby Nieuports,
Flying out to War,
Lewis guns all loaded
Engines all a-roar;
See! The Flight Commander
Leads against the foe,
Five machines with engines revving
Cylinders aglow!"

Stewart Keith Jopp ('Twenty-eight Days in France', p. 35), to the tune of the hymn 'Onward Christian Soldiers'.

The Royal Flying Corps Communiqués noted in the entry dated 19 May 1917:

> *On the evening of the 18th six machines of 1 squadron crossed the lines at about 20 feet and attacked German balloons. Two were brought down in flames; one by Lt HJ Duncan and one by 2nd Lt TH Lines. 2nd Lt WC Campbell, 1 Squadron, while on patrol, attacked a German balloon and brought it down in flames. (Bowyer, 1998, p. 56).*

The Communiqués were closed off at 6.30 pm each day, so anything that happened that evening was noted in the next day's record.

It was hoped that 1 Squadron could emulate the success that 40 Squadron had achieved with their recent surprise attack using the technique of flying in low. The order to attack six balloons immediately had come from the Wing, however, 1 Squadron's Commanding Officer, Major G.C.St P. de Dombasle was not happy as he felt that the element of surprise would be absent this time and that the Germans would be ready with increased anti-aircraft artillery. According to Keith-Jopp's 'Twenty-Eight Days in France', he was reportedly "walking up and down in a state of heated agitation".

The usual patrols were out so it was a matter of collecting any pilots who could be found in the huts or the mess. The group was led by Capt R.H. Cronyn and the other pilots were Lts P.F. Fullard and H.J. Duncan and 2/Lts. M.G. Cole, L. Drummond and T.H. Lines.[6] Their six machines were single seater Nieuport 17s and 23s.

2Lt Lindsay Drummond (Royal Military College of Canada)

Shortly after 9pm (German time), the six pilots flew in low at about 100 ft altitude as planned but, as Major de Dombasle predicted, the Germans were ready with artillery including firearms and machine guns. Despite this, as reported in the communiqué mentioned, two German balloons were destroyed by Lines and Duncan. The observer on Ballonzug 92, Vizefeldwebel Gennes, jumped successfully before his balloon was set alight after being fired upon. During the fracas, Duncan was shot in the thigh and turned his plane back.

Capt Cronyn returned to the hangar first. He had not been able to cross the lines at all due to engine trouble. Then Fullard landed his plane reporting that the balloon he had been allocated to attack had been pulled down before he could reach it. He patrolled along the trenches at 30 ft and while doing so had seen a Nieuport go down in flames, so the Squadron immediately knew there had been at least one casualty. Fullard felt the attack had been a waste of time and unwisely expressed this to Brig-Gen I.T. Webb-Bowen, the 2 Brigade Commander who had come to see them off.

Despite his injury, and the fact that his plane was badly shot up, Duncan also managed to fly back across the allied lines to safety. As night fell and the officers ate dinner in the mess they could see the lights had been left on at the aerodrome in the hope that the three missing planes might return. Eventually it became apparent that Lts Cole, Drummond and Lines would not be returning and they were reported missing in action.

The Squadron had guests: some Royal Navy Air Squadron pilots. Free drinks were issued without ration in an attempt to lift the spirits of the group. It was not within the usual culture of the RFC to be openly demonstrative regarding feelings of sorrow in these circumstances. However, there was one member of the group who would not settle. Lt Lines' best friend was a pilot named 2nd Lt W.C. Campbell. They had both arrived at 1 Squadron a month before. Campbell, aged 33, was older that many in the Squadron. He spent the evening muttering and cursing and was eventually ejected from the mess by the flight commander. The officers inside could hear him pacing angrily up and down outside ranting against the Hun. Later that evening an order was received from the Wing that there would be no more balloons attacked without orders.

The next morning officers were awoken to the sound of Campbell's plane taking off which was puzzling as he was not scheduled to leave until midday. In *Twice Vertical*, Shaw included an excerpt from Keith-Jopp's diary describing how 'next morning [Campbell] went out and shot down a balloon in revenge against orders.' According to Keith-Jopp in *Twenty-Eight Days in France*, Campbell returned to the mess and greeted him in a cheery voice. 'Hullo,' he said, 'I thought I would get up early and get a balloon for Lines.'

The Royal Flying Corps Communiqués shows this claim as '2nd Lt W.C. Campbell, 1 Squadron, while on patrol, attacked a German balloon and brought it down in flames'.

Memorial plaque to Maxwell Gerard Cole

Shaw (1971) continues, 'This incident brought about a noticeably bitter change in Campbell. He was to exact a shattering retribution for the loss of his friend before the summer was out.' Sometime later the Germans dropped a note to the Allies stating that Drummond and Cole had been killed and Lt Lines had been taken prisoner. Lt Lines remained a prisoner for the duration of the war. His plane was used by the enemy after being repainted in German colours. Lines (with Keith-Jopp) wrote about what happened after landing over enemy lines in a chapter – titled 'Prisoner' in *Great War Adventures* (Tenth Series).

Max Cole died ten days before his nineteenth birthday. He was buried by the Germans at Houthem German Cemetery. Several years later, the Cole family received a letter letting them know that his body had been reinterred at Oosttaverne Wood Cemetery.

After the war, events of that day were pieced together to give a clearer picture of what had occurred in the air. Drummond had attacked Balloon 124, coming in low then rising to 100 ft altitude in keeping with instructions. His attack was unsuccessful and he was shot at by Flakzug (Anti-aircraft Section) 93 and eventually killed when his plane crashed some distance away at Terhand.[7]

Max Cole was killed by Flakzug 4 at low altitude near Balloon 91 in Kortwilde. It was his plane that Fullard had seen go down in flames.

Rosamund Cole and baby Michael

Chapter 9

MID-1917

On 30th May 1917 Fritz wrote to Rosamund from the Grand Pump Room Hotel in Bath. He had arranged to meet three fellow officers there for a meal, but when he arrived an orderly told him that they were unable to attend. He had already signed out of dinner and couldn't go back to the mess where he normally ate, so he dined at the hotel by himself. After some cold salmon and mayonnaise followed by fruit salad, he sipped on a cup of coffee while writing his letter. He told how he had bought her a 'bit of glass' which he was going to bring back with him that Friday. He wrote how grateful he was that God had kept their 'little family alive so far' and how much he was looking forward to the baby being born then Wommie would be 'all right again'. He urged her not to worry any more than she could help.

Their son, Michael William Cole, was born on 10 June 1917. Maxwell was to have been a godfather to the new baby.

On 13th June a telegram arrived from Rosamund's brother Home (128 Battery).

> *Dearest Wommie, Best of future luck for you and your son. May he never have to go to war.*

Chapter 10

_____

MORE WAR

During 1917 two of the Cole sisters got married. Irene married Pat Baillie-Lane and Gwen married Fritz's fellow officer Harry King.

At this time Cyril was still part of 2/5th Gloucesters who formed part of the 184th Brigade, 61st (2/South Midland) Division, XI Corps, First Army. 61st Division then transferred to Arras, XIX Corps, Fifth Army. Their next major action was at the Third Battle of Ypres which is also known as the Battle of Passchendaele. On 22 August, 2/5th Battalion was involved in fierce fighting to take the concrete fortification at Pond Farm. On that day alone, three officers and sixteen other ranks were killed, one officer and fifty-one other ranks wounded and one other rank missing from the 2/5th Gloucestershire Regiment.

Passchendaele was very costly in human terms. Over 300,000 Allied and 200,000 German soldiers lost their lives in the fighting and endless rain led to the offensive being known as the 'Battle of Mud'. By then the USA had joined the war in support of the Allies.

The Division was transferred again in mid-September, back to Arras but now with XVII Corps and Third Army. It was involved in a counter-attack on 5th December recapturing a section of the line near La Vacquerie.

On 31 October 1917 Home sent another long letter to Rosamund from the front. As he didn't know her current address it was sent to Fretherne then forwarded to her at Walden Lodge, Widcombe Hill, Bath, and it mentions that Fritz is on sick leave. Home talks a lot about little Michael in a very protective way. He writes, 'I expect him to grow up a super-man strong in mind and limb and with a brain that even Galileo or Socrates would have envied.'

In early 1918 several pieces of correspondence went back and forth between army departments and Max's father, William Henry Cole. On 19 May 1917, Max had been officially listed as Missing in Action. A short time later the Germans dropped a message stating that Lts Drummond and Cole had been killed and Lt Lines had been taken prisoner. Max was buried in Houthem Military Cemetery by the Germans. On 19 June 1917, Max's army file states that a German newspaper, *Norddeutsche Allgemeine Zeitung*, had reported him as being killed and that the information was probably correct. However it would not be officially accepted yet.

On 10 August 1917 a letter officially confirming Max's death was sent to his father at Bourne House. The letter told of the message dropped by the Germans and explained that such messages were usually reliable. The letter was typewritten but a note is handwritten at the bottom stating, 'No reference to the dropped message should be made in any public announcement.'

When Maxwell was listed as Missing in Action he continued to be paid and once he was officially Killed in Action the overpayment dating back to when he went missing was required to be refunded to the army. There were a number of discrepancies on Maxwell's account. On 17 December 1917, William Henry Cole wrote:

> *Dear Sir,*
> *I don't understand why Messrs Cox and Co should want payment of 'Mess Bill' £1.4.6 May 19th to 31st as set out on enclosed seeing my son was reported killed May 18th. Kindly explain, also why the debit of £7.16.0! If this has been credited to him in error, why did they not re debit his Banking a/c with it? They still show a credit balance due to him of £21.11.0*
> *Yours truly*
> *WH Cole.*

Home wrote again to Rosamund on 19 March 1918 enquiring after the progress of his nephew and godson. He hoped 'he is showing the requisite amount of intelligence and interest in life – a complex enough problem as you'll be the first to admit.' He described being, 'shot and gassed', although at the time of writing he was five miles behind the line in a billet.

On 25 September, 1918 Home wrote again congratulating Fritz on becoming a Major. He also joked that he had been made a Captain. 'Isn't it a jar? Captain Davies, what!' He finished the letter, 'same old guerre, same old dead Huns and same old crumps.'

2/5th Gloucestershire Transport Section (Cyril Cole seated front row centre). Photograph courtesy of The Soldiers of Gloucestershire Museum

Chapter 11

APPROACHING THE ARMISTICE

During January and February 1918 Cyril's Battalion was stationed around Fresnoy. The 2/5th received substantial reinforcement as sister battalions 2/4th and 2/6th Glosters were disbanded.   They were in the second line of defence during the German Spring offensive 1918. The Germans broke through the first line but before they enveloped the second, the battalion withdrew to Beauvois before joining the rest of the 184th Brigade at Voyennes, then joining the rest of 61st Division across the Somme. They attempted to defend the canal crossing at Breuil but the Germans broke through again forcing the 2/5th to withdraw first to Crecy then Mezieres.

On 27 and 28 March, 61st Division were driven back again trying to recapture Lamotte. The attack had launched at midday, but there had been little opportunity for the 2/5th to prepare their artillery. The enemy position was strongly held with machine gun fire sweeping across the right-hand side of the men. The Battalion suffered over two hundred casualties. The men withdrew and dug in 1,000 yards to the west of Marcelcave Village. Enemy shelling continued over the next few days. The weather was very wet. On 31 March the Battalion was relieved by an Australian Company and moved to rest at Gentelles. The 2/5th was then moved back under the command of XI Corps, First Army. They arrived at Steenbeque at 5am on 12 April and had breakfast at 7.30am.   At 7.45 they were ordered to move to St Venant as soon as possible. Throughout the day the various Companies within the Battalion were posted to different positions. By 8.30pm they moved forward as ordered.

At St Floris early the next morning a message was received by telephone that the enemy was advancing. During the day the telephone lines were disconnected and the men came under heavy machine gun fire and shelling until 5.30 pm when they evacuated the forward posts. The battery ceased at 6.45pm. The Battalion was relieved by the Argyll and Sutherland Highlanders and Gordons. Only ten days later they were involved in more fierce fighting at Baquerolles Farm.

In August many reinforcements of newly drafted soldiers joined the Battalion. There was a high sickness rate. The 2/5th Gloucesters' final battle was experienced during the Battle of Valenciennes in the area of Maresches and St Hubert in the first week of November. The hold on Maresches was maintained and on 2 November three German officers and two hundred and forty other ranks were taken prisoner. Also captured were German weapons including twenty-one machine guns. The 2/5th were relieved by the 13th Battalion Middlesex Regiment at 7pm and they arrived at their billets for the night at 9pm.

The wedding of Mr and Mrs C.L. Cole, 23 November 1918. Standing: Fritz Cole, Rosamund Cole, Unknown, Unknown, Unknown, Mr W.H. Cole, Mrs Cole Unknown, Unknown. Front: Unknown, Elsie, Cyril, One of the Cole sisters (possibly Gwen)

On 11 November 1918 the Armistice was signed and the First World War came to an end. Since early 1916 Cyril had been a Transport Officer with the 2/5th Gloucestershire Regiment. Shortly after the Armistice Cyril Cole and Elsie Kathleen Williams-White were married.

Cyril then returned to France to help with demobilisation. Unfortunately an influenza epidemic swept the world at this time. By May 1919 it had killed 20 million people – more than the 8 million killed by the war. For unknown reasons it affected young, healthy people much more than children or the elderly. Tragically, one of these was Cyril, who died of bronchial pneumonia in March 1919.

A.F. Barnes wrote in The Story of the 2/5th Battalion Gloucestershire Regiment 1914–1918,

> *The transport officers whom the Battalion best remembers were Capt. Cyril Cole, Lieut. Bright and Lieut. Davis. Capt. Cole went through the War and then became a victim to the influenza scourge that raged through Europe after the Armistice.*

The handwritten draft copy of the obituary for Cyril Lawson Cole reads:

> *A brilliant and useful career has been brought to an untimely end by the death, in the service of his King and country of Captain Cyril Lawson Cole. He was the second son of W.H. Cole, Esq, J.P., and of Mrs Cole of Bourne House, Brimscombe, Gloucestershire and was born in Cirencester on October 10th 1892. He was educated at Morton Hall, Worcestershire and at Marlborough College, where he had a successful career, proving himself a sound scholar and good all round sportsman. At the age of twenty he entered Glasgow University and obtained his Bachelor of Science degree being afterwards apprenticed at the celebrated Fairfield Ship Building Yards in Glasgow. The outbreak of the Great War brought an immediate response to the call of duty and he was almost immediately granted a Commission as Sec.-Lieutenant in the Gloucestershire Regiment. Early in 1916 he was sent to France where he served till the end. He was frequently in action and showed himself a cool and fearless soldier and a capable leader of men. With the conclusion of the Armistice he looked forward to resuming his civil career and on November 23rd, 1918 he married Elsie Kathleen, only daughter of Frederick Williams-White, Esq., of Hampstead. Captain Cole returned to the front and was attached to the 184th Infantry Brigade Headquarters when he was attacked by the prevalent disease which*

wrought such havoc both at home and abroad in the winter of 1918 – 1919 and the following spring. He was taken to No. 20 General Hospital at Camiers, where, on March 14th, he died from bronchial pneumonia and on March 16th was buried with full military honours in Etaples Cemetery. His death was deeply felt by all who knew him, and most of all by his parents who had already lost their two younger sons in the Cause. The country greatly needs the services of all these patriots at this crisis and deeply as we must regret the death of so many brave men in the high and holy cause of their King and Country, we must measure our loss, not only in the gallant lives which have been so nobly laid down, but in the crying need we more than ever experience for the services of those who should now be ready to carry on the work of the Nation. We can only trust that the record of their deeds may raise up others to emulate their actions.

Ivor Gurney (1890–1937), 2/5th Gloucestershire Battalion, was one of the First World War's most celebrated poets. His poem 'Question and Answer' is a poignant reminder of the loss of many sons.

Question and Answer

What shall I say, O soldiers unforgotten
And friends most dear, but fallen, when they shall ask
'How died our sons that were in pain begotten,
Whose boyhood's making was our daily task?

And what have you to comfort our most lonely
Our undivided anguish, what word to tell?'
Soldiers, what can be said, what told but only
'Your work was nobly ended: they died well.'

EPILOGUE

Campbell and Fullard went on to become No. 1 Squadron's highest scoring aces of the First World War. Major W.C. Campbell DSO, MC and Bar had a particular inclination for attacking balloons and Capt. P.F. Fullard DSO, MC and Bar developed an aversion to them after the events of 18 May 1917.

Edward 'Mick' Mannock became 40 Squadron's most successful Royal Flying Corps pilot. Major Mick Mannock received a posthumous VC.

THE COLE FAMILY AFTER THE WAR

In June 1919 Fritz was awarded his MBE. He returned to the family business after the war but the Great Depression meant that business held more challenges than before. Fritz, Rosamund, son Michael and daughter Penelope (born in April 1920) moved to The Limes in Benson, Oxfordshire, chosen because it was halfway between the business premises in Brimscombe and the customers in London.

Sadly, Home's wish that his godson, Michael (Mick to the family) 'never go to war', was not granted. As he was in the Naval Reserve, he was called up by the Royal Navy during the Second World War. In 1942, he lost his infant son, Raymond, to enteritis contracted on the crowded evacuee boat in which Mick's wife, Anne, and the baby were fleeing Singapore. Mick and Anne eventually had two daughters.

Fritz was a popular man in the village of Benson and the wider neighbourhood. All reports suggest he got along well with people. During the Second World War he led the Special Constabulary in Oxfordshire and for many years he was a committed Freemason and the Church Warden of St Helen's Church, Benson, in whose churchyard he is buried. At the time of his death he was survived by his wife Rosamund, children Michael and Penelope, and four grandchildren.

Fritz died prematurely in 1955 and his son Mick believed it may have been as a result of his time in the trenches. Mick said that for many of those soldiers, health problems showed themselves years later. Two years after Fritz' death, the family was to suffer further tragedy when Penelope was killed in a car accident.

The Cole Sisters - As previously mentioned, Gwen married Harry King and Irene married Pat Lane. In 1923, Phyllis married Richard Dawkins.

Medals of Major F.W. Cole

Major F.W. Cole (c.1950)

Elsie Kathleen Williams-White - Cyril's widow was to experience further turmoil. Elsie was born on 17th December 1892 at Taunton, Somerset and married Cyril Lawson Cole on 23rd November 1918 at Westhampnett, Sussex. After Cyril's death she married George Christopher Stead on 21st July 1921 at Hampstead Parish Church, Hampstead, Middlesex. Elsie and George had a son, Peter George Stead, who was born in 1923. In 1930, George Christopher Stead petitioned for divorce, the co-respondent was a Norman James Macdonald. Elsie and Norman married in 1931. Sadly, her son Peter died in 1934 aged ten. Elsie died in Devon in 1977.

Brian Spearing Cole - Shortly after the war there was a court case, Cole v. Cole, to determine whether Brian was entitled to a share of the estate of his father, Caleb Bruce Cole. At first glance this appears to be a family disagreement but a reading of the judgement shows that in fact the court was approached to clarify a point of law. Brian was to inherit a substantial number of shares of H.J. Packer and Co. Ltd from his father on the condition that he was employed there from the age of twenty until the age of thirty-three. He worked there as a clerk from the age of eighteen until 15 September 1914 when he voluntarily enlisted in His Majesty's Forces. The court case was to clarify whether he resigned from his employment at H.J. Packer or was on temporary leave during his time at war. The court found, quite rightly, that he was granted a temporary dispensation by the directors and that although he did not render service to the company he was still employed by them during this time.

William and Kitty - Both died in 1932. The elder members of the family relate that Kitty was never the same after losing her sons.

Michael William Cole - Died in 2009 aged ninety-two. He is survived by his wife Mrs Kay Cole, daughters Anita and Annie, five grandchildren and five great-grandchildren.

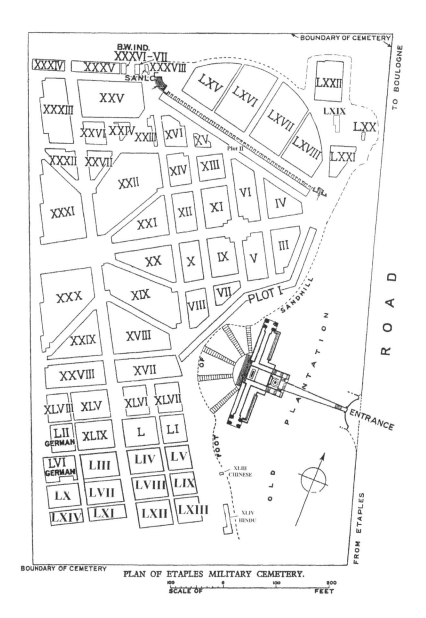

Plan of Etaples Military Cemetery (Commonwealth War Graves Commission)

HOW TO VISIT THE COLE BROTHERS

Four of us flew out of Exeter on a crisp summer's day in June 2012. After only an hour our plane landed in Paris at Charles de Gaulle Airport. All passengers were loaded on to a bus and driven to the terminus to be processed through customs. There were several hundred passengers and very few customs officers, our wait in the queue took longer than our flight from the UK. Finally, overjoyed, we reached the front of the queue and the officer asked me how long I was staying in France. Determined to reply in French, I summoned up my high school knowledge and recent studies yet completely forgot how to count. I counted out my fingers on the counter: 'un, deux, trios', and he said, 'Oh you've come here to play the piano!' Finally we were through customs and it was time to pick up the rental car. It didn't take long to get used to driving on the other side of the road again and we had a sat nav that helped a lot. We drove directly to Etaples Military Cemetery where Cyril is buried. The cemetery and gardens are pristine and very well cared for. It is one of the biggest in France because the hospital in Etaples had previously been an army training base. He was the only one of the Cole brothers to have a formal military funeral. I had previously found out the grave numbers and had a plan of the cemetery, so it was relatively easy to find him. His grave is numbered XLV.C.14. There is a message on the gravestone from his young wife. It reads 'I thank God for every Remembrance of You – Elsie'. I wrote a message in the book provided at the entrance.

Having not made any plans for accommodation that night we winged it, travelling along all sorts of interesting streets then driving further up the coast. We pulled into a town called Gravelines at about 5.30pm and went to the marina for a coffee. There we found a very useful information desk with details of amenities in the area including Hotel de Beffroi in Place Charles-Valentin. Our group of four turned up without a booking and they offered us rooms at a very reasonable rate. The rooms were clean and had all we needed. The highlight of our stay in this delightful town was our meal at Le Queen Mary around the corner. It was full of locals, which is always a good sign. The hosts were friendly, coped well with our appalling French and served excellent food. The entertaining waiter could not stop collapsing in hysterics each time he saw us due to us asking for a potato instead of apple juice. There is a difference between 'pomme' and 'pomme de terre'. We enjoyed a walk after dinner, the canals surrounding the town are really something else. I'm amazed Gravelines is not a more famous tourist attraction because it was such a lovely town. We hope to return one day.

The next morning after noticing a queue out the door of the nearby Blas Boulangerie Patisserie and buying some decadent cakes and treats, we set off for Belgium. There is an open border but one could instantly see the change in language on the road signs. We got lost. As we drove further into the countryside we saw a sight that made us stop in the middle of the road. A Belgian Blue bull. We had never seen so much testosterone in all our lives. After taking several photographs we were on our way again. We felt that we had driven

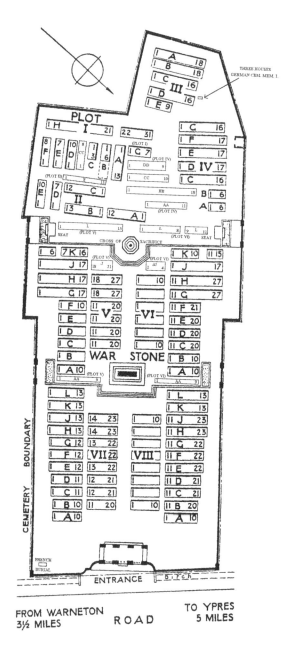

Plan of Oosttaverne Military Cemetery

past our destination and stopped at a shop where we sought directions from two young women who didn't speak French. Neither did we, but our pidgen French was better than our non-existent Flemish. Never mind, we bought lots of posh lollies from them. When travelling around Europe the Euro, as opposed to multiple currencies, is very useful. After backtracking, we knocked on the door of a helpful stranger who offered directions. The cemetery at Oosttaverne was much smaller but equally well cared for. Max, buried in grave number I.H.19 was near the back tucked in at the edge. His gravestone reads that he was nineteen but that's incorrect. The authorities probably took it off the literal year – he was still eighteen when he was killed.

We drove back to France to visit the final Cole brother, Clifford; and the graveyard he was in was even smaller. There are many very small Commonwealth cemeteries in this area. We had difficulty with the sat nav because of some roadworks, but we got to see more of the country and interesting architecture. Laventie is a very green and picturesque part of the country. Once we were on the correct road at Laventie the cemetery was easy to find. Clifford died in the trenches after only one month in France. He was an officer and is buried next to several other men from his regiment who died later the same week in June 1916. His grave number is II.J.5. The four of us paid our respects to him (as we had to the other two boys) then continued on our journey.

We headed south to make some headway towards Paris to shorten the journey the next day. We were very hungry by then and previously unaware that this part of France appears to completely shut down on a Sunday. There wasn't a shop, supermarket or any way, of buying food. Eventually we asked a local and discovered the A L'Potee d'Leandre on 107 rue Pasteur in Souchez. The hosts were tidying up after a private function and the kitchen was closing, but they saw our predicament and generously made us some huge delicious salads and cold meats. We were very grateful to them for their gracious hospitality.

Replenished, we headed for Arras. We shopped around for accommodation as we simply wanted somewhere clean and affordable to sleep for the night before returning to Paris the next morning. La Belle Etoile on ZA Les Alouettes was perfect for what we needed. The hotel restaurant was closed but reception gave us very good advice to eat dinner at the nearby Café Leffe. It was a sunny late Sunday afternoon with a buoyant and busy atmosphere in the town square. Again we strolled the streets after our evening meal.

The next morning we rose early and drove to Paris where we spent three unforgettable days exploring the city and staying at the Hotel du Nord, 47 rue Albert Thomas.

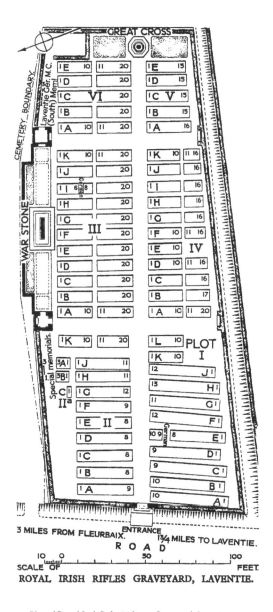

Plan of Royal Irish Rifles Military Graveyard, Laventie

NOTES

1. The Rev C.P. Davies was a Fellow of the Royal Astronomical Society and was also a renowned campanologist.

2. Thomas Mudge invented the detached lever escapement still found in all pocket watches today and received a financial award from the Board of Longitude for his research and contributions to keeping time at sea. Several of his clocks and watches can be found in London at the British Museum and at the National Maritime Museum at Greenwich.

3. Brian was a 2nd Lieutenant in 1914 with the 12th Battalion, The Gloucestershire Regiment. Records show that he trained in England with RFC 66 Squadron in late 1916. After recovering from his first crash on 17 January 1917, he was wounded in action a second time on 27 March 1918 while flying a Sopwith Dolphin with 79 Squadron in France.

4. Surname changed by author.

5. Grenade.

6. Lt H.J. Duncan was flying Nieuport plane number A6619, 2/Lt M.G. Cole B1555, Lt. L. Drummond B1636 and Lt. T.H. Lines N6644.

7. Canadian Lt L. Drummond was nicknamed 'Linley' or 'Drummie'. He was known as a practical joker and gifted photographer (Royal Military College of Canada, 2007). Originally in France as an observer due to his photography skills, he returned to England to train as a pilot in late 1916; he had only arrived at 1 Squadron in April 1917. His body was never recovered. He was twenty-four years old and is remembered with honour on the Arras Flying Services Memorial in France.

RECOMMENDED READING

A Tommy's Sketchbook by Lance-Corporal Henry Buckle, edited by David Read, is an excellent record of what life was like in the trenches in 1915 for 1/5th Gloucestershire Regiment. It includes diary excerpts and many hand-drawn sketches.

The Story of the 2/5th Battalion Gloucestershire Regiment 1914 – 1918, written by A.F. Barnes in 1930, is an in-depth and thorough account of the experiences of this Regiment during the Great War.

Twice Vertical and *No. 1 Squadron*, by Michael Shaw, relate the history of the Royal Flying Corps No. 1 Squadron, which later became Royal Air Force No. 1 Squadron.

'Twenty-Eight Days in France', by Stewart Keith-Jopp, magazine article, *Great War Adventures,* Ninth Series gives a wonderful description of what life was like for No. 1 Squadron in Bailleul in 1917.

'Prisoner', by T.H. Lines and S. Keith-Jopp, magazine article, *Great War Adventures,* Tenth Series, relates the story of what happened to Lines after his plane was shot down and he was taken prisoner by the Germans.

Nieuports in RNAS, RFC and RAF Service, by Cross and Cockade International, is an incredible monograph of Nieuport planes.

Wings, the complete BBC series is available on DVD. It shows what life was like for pilots in the Royal Flying Corps.

BIBLIOGRAPHY

Barnes MC, A. (1930). *The story of the 2/5th Battalion Gloucestershire Regiment 1914–1918.* Gloucester: The Crypt House Press.

Bickers, R.T. (1988). *The First Great Air War.* London: Hodder and Stoughton.

Bowyer, C. (1998). *Royal Flying Corps Communiqué 1917–1918.* London: Grub Street.

Buckle, H. (2012). *A Tommy's Sketchbook: Writings and Drawings from the Trenches.* (D. Read, Ed.) Stroud: The History Press.

Gurney, I. (1984). *Ivor Gurney War Letters: A Selection.* (R. Thornton, Ed.) London: Hogarth.

Harvey, F. (1917). *Gloucester Friends: Poems from a German Prison Camp.* London: Sidgwick and Jackson.

Keith-Jopp, S. (date unknown). 'Twenty-Eight Days in France'. *Great War Adventures: Thrilling Experiences of Soldiers, Sailors and Airmen* (Ninth Series), pp. 35–60.

Lines, T. H., and Keith-Jopp, S. (date unknown). 'Prisoner'. *Great War Adventures*, (Tenth Series), pp. 112–116.

McDarment, C. (1931). 'With the Balloon Busters'. *Popular Mechanics*, 55 (5).

O'Connor, M. (1982). 'P.F. Fullard: Nieuport Exponent'. *Cross and Cockade Great Britain Journal*, 63 - 69.

Oughton, F.(ed.) (1966). *The Personal Diary of Major Edward 'Mick' Mannock. V.C., D.S.O. (2 bars), M.C. (1 bar). Royal Flying Corps and Royal Air Force.* London: Neville Spearman.

Powell, A. (2006). *The Fierce Light: The Battle of the Somme July–November 1916.* Stroud: Sutton Publishing.

Royal Military College of Canada. (2007). *The Stone Frigate 1914.* Acessed 7 August 2010, from www.archive.org: http://www.archive.org/details/stonefrigate191400kinguoft

Shaw, M. (1971). *Twice Vertical: The History of No. 1 squadron Royal Air Force.* London: Macdonald and Co.

Lightning Source UK Ltd.
Milton Keynes UK
UKOW06f1820111114

241466UK00012B/670/P